Walter
and the
Mucous Monsters

This book is dedicated to the families of kids with Cystic Fibrosis. In hopes that they are as supportive and encouraging as Walter's family has always been.

Thank you
Herman, Connie and Frank

Thank you to the families of the team-members for supporting their loved ones who cycled with Walter.

And special thanks to the Adult CF Unit of the Royal Hobart Hospital in Tasmania for their knowledge, care and patience.

www.coughingthedistance.com
katherine@coughingthedistance.com

This is Walter. He lives in Tasmania, Australia.

This is the story of how Walter rode his bicycle from Paris, France to Istanbul, Turkey.

His journey would cover 11 countries, travelling over 4000 kilometres, taking 72 days. It was especially challenging because Walter has Cystic Fibrosis.

When Walter was only ten years old, doctors told him and his family that he has Cystic Fibrosis. He was born with it, and there is no cure.

The whole family was very sad, knowing Walter's health would get worse.

Walter was not worried. He knows having Cystic Fibrosis makes him very special.

He has trouble breathing because his lungs fill up with sticky mucous.

To defeat these Mucous Monsters, they need to be coughed out, every day.

This makes Walter like a super-hero.

Everyone knows that coughing spreads germs, and spitting is gross and naughty. But this is how Walter fights the Mucous Monsters.

He discovered that riding his bike and running in the forests are great ways to stay healthy, and stay out of trouble!

Walter also discovered he needs to eat loads of food to stay strong.

Cystic Fibrosis makes it hard for his body to digest all this food properly, so he needs to take special pills with every meal.

If he doesn't, Walter gets pains in his stomach, terrible diarrhoea and really stinky farts!

After many years fighting the Mucous Monsters
and taking good care of himself, 42 year old Walter
decided he would have a great adventure.

He told his doctor that he hoped to ride
his bicycle across Europe.
Dr Reid was very impressed! "You will
inspire other people", he said,
"and you can tell lots of people about
Cystic Fibrosis".

So, Walter, the CF super-hero, started training for his big adventure.

Every day he rode his bike further, and further. He was coughing more and more each day.

Walter uses a nebuliser to defeat the Mucous Monsters. He breathes medicine into his lungs to help him cough. He would need to be very strong and healthy.

Every super-hero needs help.
Walter put together a great team of friends to
join the ride from Paris to Istanbul.

David is from Canberra, he is a policeman who
used to be a paramedic. He is "Doc Cop",
and was put in charge of
navigation and first aid.

David
"Doc Cop"

Troy

Troy is a mechanic from Tasmania. He would drive
the support car with everyone's clothes and food,
and Walter's medicine.

Troy could fix anything that
broke down or blew up.
He was excited about driving on the other side
of the road.

Heather is a journalist from Canada.
She joined the ride to take pictures and
write about what happened along the way.
She loves climbing, skiing and rafting,
but cycling long distances was a new challenge.

Heather   **Lucas**

Lucas is a film-maker from Canberra.
He would have a camera in his hand all the time,
even when riding his bicycle.
Lucas would make a movie called
"Coughing the Distance",
starring a Cystic Fibrosis super-hero,
named Walter, riding his bicycle across Europe,
whilst fighting the Mucous Monsters.

9

Walter was very happy to have such a great team. Other friends joined the ride in different places.

Martin came from Holland to let the team use his car as their support vehicle.

Cindy came from Tasmania to give haircuts and lots of encouragement.

Brent and his 7 year old son, **Niki**, came from America for a few days of riding in Europe.

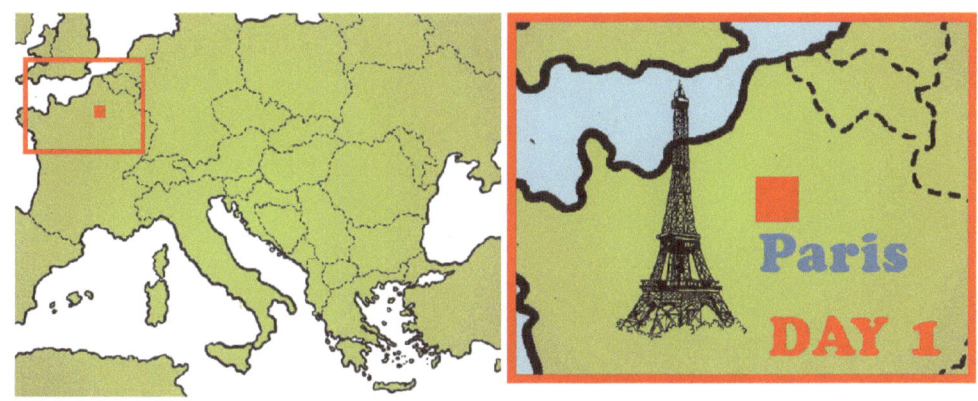

After months of training and preparation,
it was time to start the adventure!

On 28th July 2007, Walter and his team gathered
on their bicycles under the Eiffel Tower.

"3- 2 -1, GO!" said Walter.

The team started their ride, following the same route as the **Tour de France**.

Staying together and riding long distances was very challenging. Each person had a special, important role, and everyone had to keep up and stay together.

Lucas was getting used to filming and riding his bicycle at the same time when he had a **crash**!

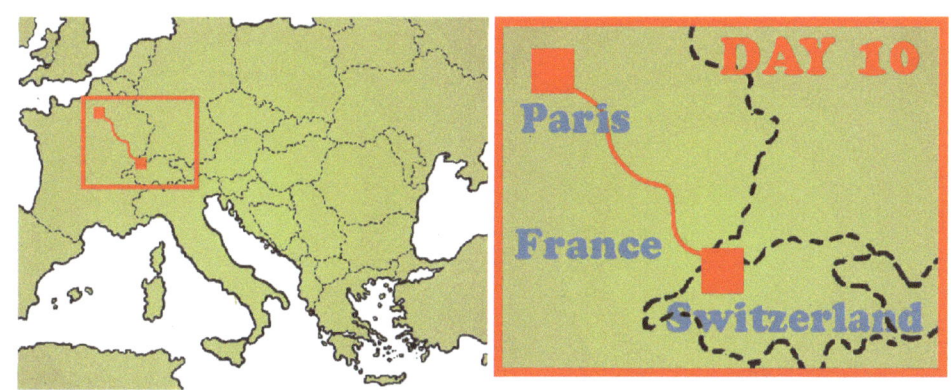

Walter's job was to stay healthy and keep battling the Mucous Monsters.

On the way to Germany, they rode through Switzerland in one day!

There are lots of hills in this part of Europe, and Walter climbed each one slowly and steadily. Then he raced down the other side, coughing out Mucous Monsters all the way.

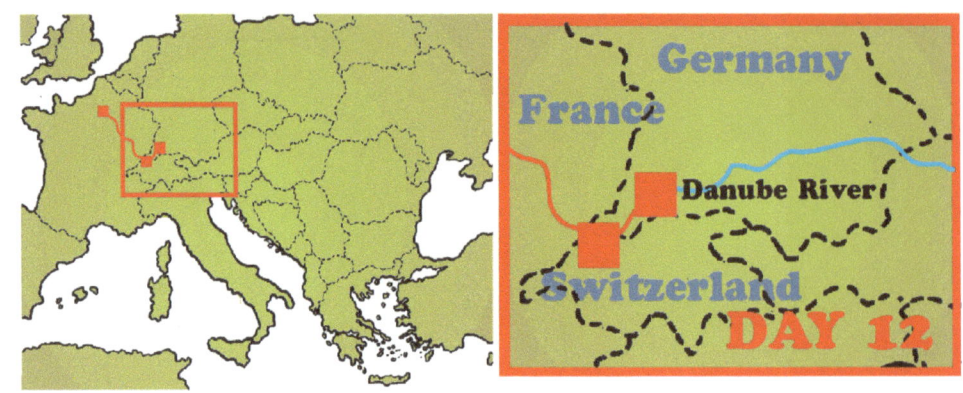

The terrain became flatter and the riding easier along the Danube River.

Walter was becoming more fit with all this riding. But, there was pollution in the air, and many people smoking in restaurants where the team were eating.

This made the Mucous Monsters angry and strong. Walter needed a rest day, but although he felt unwell, this CF super-hero was determined to ride on.

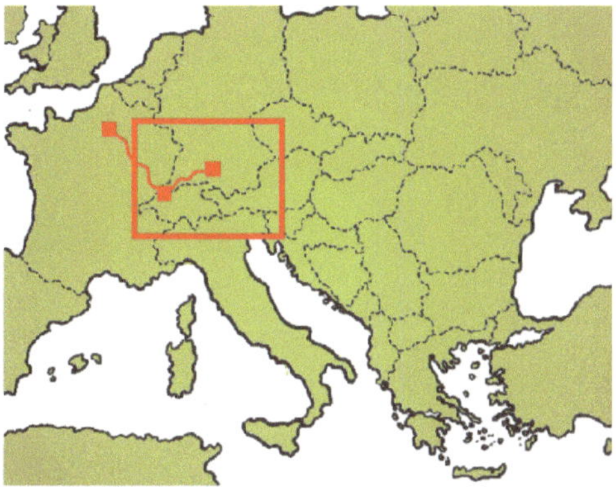

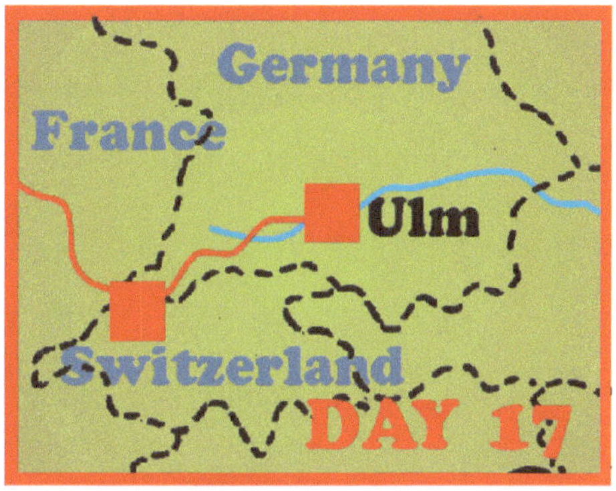

DAY 17

(Map labels: Germany, France, Switzerland, Ulm)

Arriving in Ulm, Germany, the team celebrated: they had already ridden over 1000 kilometres!

But they worried about Walter, he was not himself. The Mucous Monsters were now very big and ugly.

Walter needed more antibiotics. He had more pills and was breathing antibiotics through his nebuliser.

Walter was fighting the Mucous Monsters with everything he had.

15

Walter was worried...
What if he could not make it?
What if the antibiotics didn't work this time?
What if he had to go to hospital?
And so far from home!

But **super-heroes** don't give up,
Walter kept riding.

His team was very supportive.
The **medicine** started to work.

By **day 22**, Walter was winning the battle
with the **Mucous Monsters**.
He was feeling much better as
the team rode in to **Austria**.

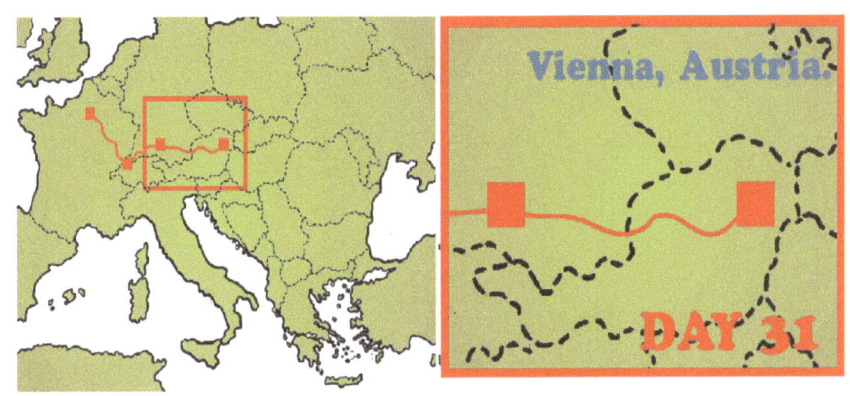

The team celebrated Walter's triumph over
the Mucous Monsters.
They heard music composed by Mozart
at the Vienna Opera House.

Everyone was happy to finally have
a rest for a couple of days!

Cindy met up with the team in Vienna.
They were glad to have a new team member
for the next part of the journey.

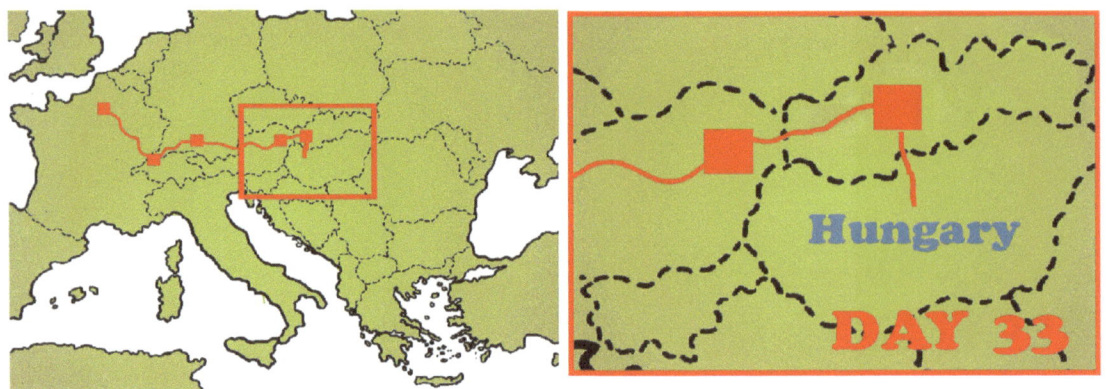

Walter and the team picked up the pace.
They traveled through Slovakia and
into Hungary in one day!

Walter had the Mucous Monsters
well under control now.
In the morning, at the start of riding,
he would cough and spit a lot.

In the evening he had a mighty appetite.
Being in Hungary made Walter hungry!

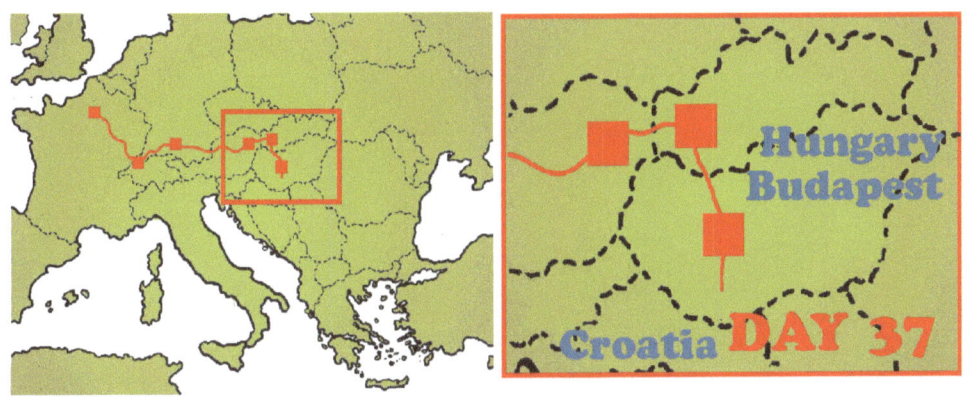

When they arrived in beautiful Budapest,
the team celebrated reaching halfway
on their big adventure.

Then they rode through Croatia and Serbia.
They saw many buildings filled with
bullet holes from the recent war.

Walter the CF super-hero thought
how glad he was to have only his
Mucous Monsters to fight.

Riding through Serbia and Croatia became harder.
There were no bike paths to follow.
Walter was busy coughing, keeping up
and trying to look like a super-hero
as Lucas filmed him.

The team had completed almost 3000 kilometres
as they rode in to Romania.

Travelling through **Romania**, Walter was feeling healthy and strong. The team were riding up to **140 kilometres every day!**

It was a challenge to find their way. The road signs are not written in **English**, and the letters of the **Romanian** alphabet are different. Nobody could understand the signs!

David led the way brilliantly, using his maps and **GPS** (global positioning system).

Troy was busy in Romania. He helped Cindy fix a flat tyre. He had to change brake pads, tighten brake and gear cables, oil chains and fix anything that had broken.

Troy saved the day when the car fridge stopped working. Walter's medicine could have been ruined. Troy fixed it with a piece of foil from a chewing gum wrapper!

Walter was chased by a pack of
angry Romanian dogs.
He wished his lungs were stronger so
he could go faster and get away.
Luckily, he wasn't bitten and the dogs
were left behind with some Mucous Monsters.

It seemed the harder he pushed himself,
the more he could cough.

The team reached **Constanta**, on the Black Sea.

They rode past a sign for **fried chicken**
on the way into town.
They were hungry and tried asking for directions.
But they couldn't speak **Romanian**,
and could find no one who spoke **English**.

So they searched, for hours,
until they found the restaurant!

They all enjoyed a picnic on the beach.

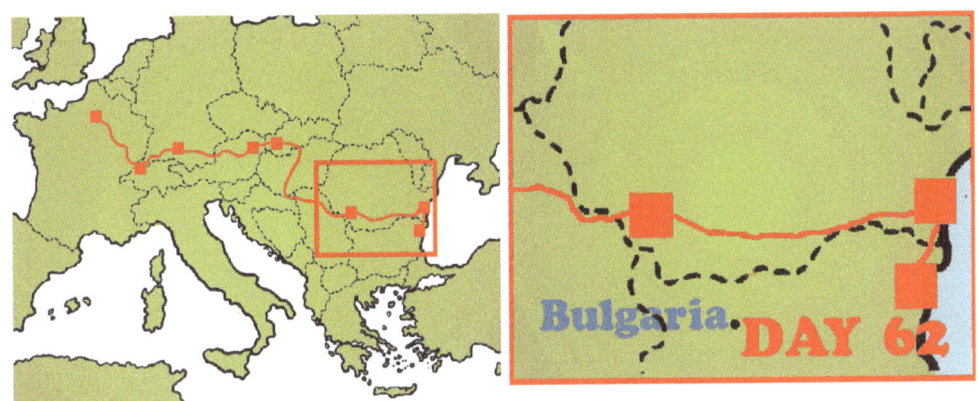

The team rode in to the seaside town
of Balcik, Bulgaria.
They had a couple of days to rest before
the final push into Turkey.
It was a beautiful place, and Walter was
feeling well and strong.
The Mucous Monsters were not being
so troublesome now.

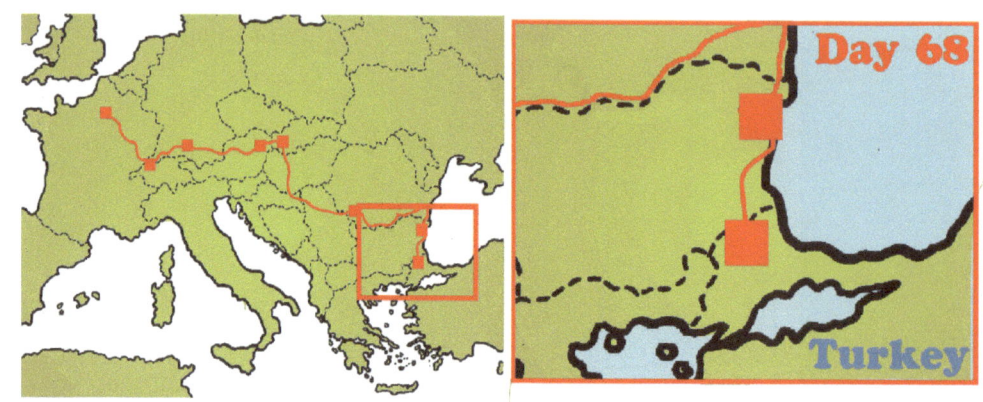

Walter and the team rode up and down
many hills as they arrived in Turkey.

They stopped for an
overnight stay in Pinarhisar.
Everyone had been looking forward
to a warm shower and comfortable bed
after all the hard riding.
But there are no hotels
in this part of Turkey,
so the team had to camp out, again!

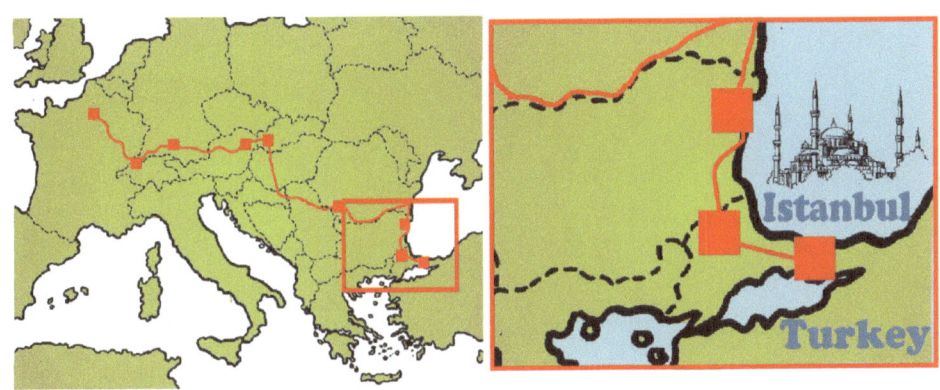

Finally!

72 Days after starting out from the Eiffel Tower, Walter the CF super-hero, and his wonderful team, arrived in Istanbul!

It had taken just over 10 weeks to ride more than 4000 kilometres!

The team was welcomed as heroes
as they rode in to the Dutch consulate.

A brass band was playing, and Walter
was given a huge bunch of flowers.
There was a big party,
with lots of delicious food.

Everyone congratulated Walter,
"what a great feat you have accomplished".

And that's the story of how
Walter the CF super-hero
cycled across Europe.

He knows that the secret to success
is to always trust in your super-hero self.
And surround yourself with friends
who believe in you.

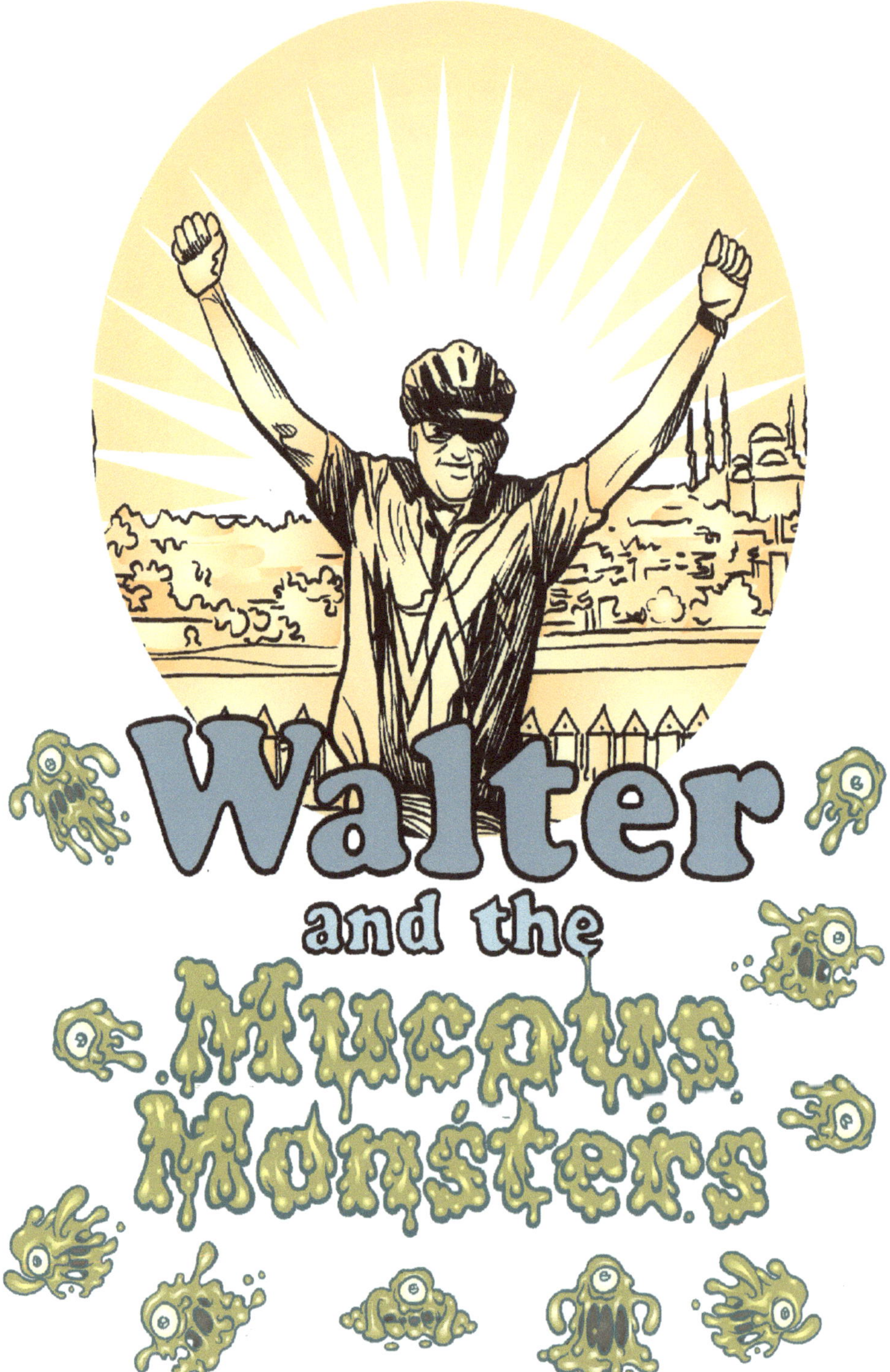

Proudly supported by

Cystic Fibrosis

Cystic Fibrosis Tasmania

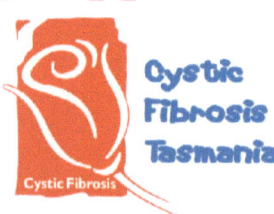

www.ingramcontent.com/pod-product-compliance
Lightning Source LLC
Chambersburg PA
CBHW060806290526

45792CB00005BA/1539